My Pony Book

Dawn McMillan

Contents

My Pony

Flash is my pony.

He is a good pet.

It is fun to ride!

A pony is a little horse.

horse

pony

Look at the parts of a pony.

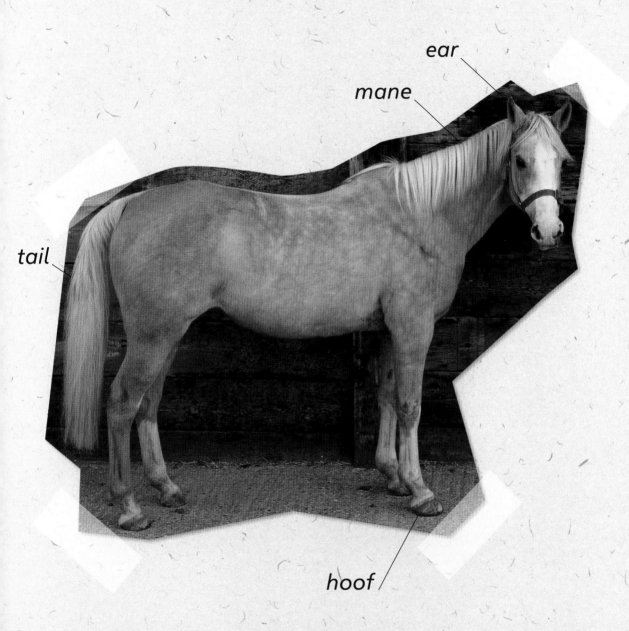

ear

mane

tail

hoof

5

Looking after My Pony

I like to look after Flash.

I brush Flash with this brush.

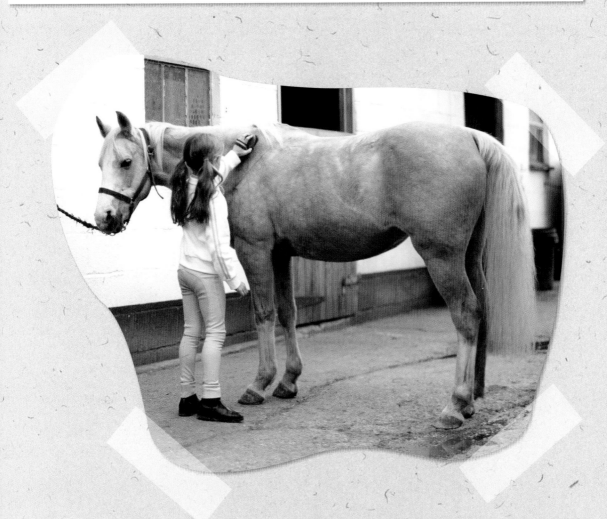

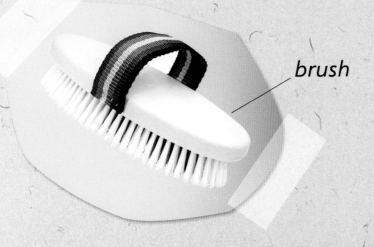

brush

I clean his feet with a hoof pick.

horse shoe

hoof

A pony's foot is a hoof.

hoof pick

Look! This is Flash's field.

I get Flash some food.

chaff

hay

water

I get Flash some water, too.

I Like to Ride

I like to ride Flash.

I put on a hard hat.

We had fun!

Flash did well.
We got a ribbon!

Things to Do for Flash

- Brush Flash and clean his feet.

- Ride Flash.

- Get Flash food and water.

- Hug Flash!